# COOKING
# FOR COMPANY

The following Canadian companies were involved in the production
of this Collection: Colour Technologies, Fred Bird & Associates Limited,
Gordon Sibley Design Inc., On-line Graphics, Telemedia Publishing Inc. and
The Madison Book Group Inc.

Canadian Living is a trademark of Telemedia Publishing Inc.
All trademark rights, registered and unregistered, are reserved.

We acknowledge the contribution of
Drew Warner, Joie Warner and Flavor Publications.

**Produced by**
**The Madison Book Group Inc.**
**40 Madison Avenue**
**Toronto, Ontario**
**Canada**
**M5R 2S1**

# COOKING FOR COMPANY

■ *On our cover:*
*Rosemary Lamb*
*Chops (p. 26)*

I f you panic every time you have to entertain, relax! We've taken the fuss and worry out of planning any social occasion, with 55 appealing and delicious recipes that make it easy to entertain with flair. Whether it's a special dinner for four or a relaxed summer gathering around the patio, you'll find recipes here to suit every taste and every mood — from satisfying appetizers like *Pork Satays with Plum Sauce* or down-home *Crunchy Parmesan Chicken Wings* to effortless main-dish courses like *Rosemary Lamb Chops* or savory *Pork Roast with Apples*. We've also included a seasonal selection of pleasing desserts like *Rhubarb Sour Cream Crunch Pie* and cool *Lemon Cream Pavé* — plus make-ahead shortcuts, serving suggestions and garnishing tips throughout.

**Cooking for Company** is just one of the eight full-color cookbooks that make up THE CANADIAN LIVING COOKING COLLECTION. Inside each of these colorful cookbooks are the kind of satisfying, easy-to-make dishes you'll want to cook over and over again. Each recipe in the Collection has been carefully selected and tested by *Canadian Living* to make sure it turns out wonderfully every time you make it. When you collect all eight cookbooks, you can choose from over 500 dishes — from marvelous soups to sensational desserts — all guaranteed to make any meal extra special.

*Elizabeth Baird*

**Elizabeth Baird**
**Food Director,** *Canadian Living* **Magazine**

# Savory Appetizer Pie

*Cut this delicious appetizer pie into squares and serve on small plates with a fork. It's a perfect dish for holiday entertaining or any special occasion.*

### CRUST

| | | |
|---|---|---|
| 4 cups | coarse fresh bread crumbs | 1 L |
| 2/3 cup | freshly grated Parmesan cheese | 150 mL |
| 1/2 cup | butter, melted | 125 mL |

### FILLING

| | | |
|---|---|---|
| 2 cups | ricotta or cream cheese | 500 mL |
| 1/2 cup | freshly grated Parmesan cheese | 125 mL |
| 1 | egg | 1 |
| 2 tbsp | minced fresh parsley | 25 mL |
| 1/2 tsp | salt | 2 mL |
| 1/2 tsp | dried basil | 2 mL |
| Pinch | pepper | Pinch |

### TOPPING

| | | |
|---|---|---|
| 2 cups | broccoli florets | 500 mL |
| 1 cup | cauliflower florets | 250 mL |
| 1/4 lb | smoked salmon | 125 g |
| Quarter | English cucumber, peeled and sliced | Quarter |
| 4 | mushrooms, sliced | 4 |
| 4 | black olives, quartered | 4 |
| 7 | cherry tomatoes, quartered | 7 |
| 2 tbsp | black lumpfish caviar | 25 mL |
| 1 tsp | capers | 5 mL |

■ **Crust:** On baking sheet, toast crumbs in 350°F (180°C) oven for 10 to 15 minutes or until golden, stirring once. Transfer to bowl; stir in cheese and butter. Pat firmly into 11- × 8-inch (28 × 20 cm) tart pan with removable bottom. Bake in 350°F (180°C) oven until golden, about 10 minutes.

■ **Filling:** In bowl, beat together ricotta, Parmesan, egg, parsley, salt, basil and pepper until smooth; spoon into crust, smoothing top. Bake for 20 to 25 minutes or until set and tip of pointed knife inserted into centre comes out clean. Let cool on rack. *(Recipe can be prepared to this point, covered and chilled for up to 24 hours.)*

■ **Topping:** Up to 2 hours before serving, blanch broccoli and cauliflower in boiling water for 1 minute. Refresh under cold water; drain and pat dry. Cut salmon into bite-size strips. In diagonal rows, attractively arrange broccoli, cauliflower, salmon, cucumber, mushrooms, olives, tomatoes and caviar over filling. Garnish with capers. Cover and refrigerate until serving. Makes about 20 appetizers.

# Potato Pancakes with Shrimp and Dill

*Serve this wonderful appetizer three pancakes per plate with a dollop of sour cream.*

| | | |
|---|---|---|
| 3 | potatoes (1-1/4 lb/625 g total) | 3 |
| 3 | eggs | 3 |
| 2/3 cup | all-purpose flour | 150 mL |
| 1 tsp | baking powder | 5 mL |
| 1 tsp | salt | 5 mL |
| 1/2 tsp | pepper | 2 mL |
| 3 tbsp | butter, melted | 50 mL |
| 1-1/3 cups | light cream | 325 mL |
| 1 cup | cooked baby shrimp | 250 mL |
| 3 tbsp | chopped fresh dill | 50 mL |
| 1/3 cup | (approx) unsalted butter | 75 mL |

■ Peel potatoes and cut into quarters; cook in saucepan of boiling salted water until tender. Drain well and mash until smooth to make 2 cups (500 mL). Transfer to bowl and let cool.

■ In separate bowl, beat eggs; blend in flour, baking powder, salt and pepper. Whisk in melted butter and cream; gradually whisk into cool mashed potatoes. Pat shrimp very dry; stir into potato mixture along with dill.

■ In large skillet, melt 1 tbsp (15 mL) of the unsalted butter over medium heat; pour in rounded tablespoonfuls (15 mL) batter for each pancake, about 4 inches (10 cm) apart. Cook for 3 to 4 minutes or until tiny bubbles appear on surface and underside is golden. Turn and cook for 1 to 1-1/2 minutes longer or until golden.

■ Transfer pancakes to platter and keep warm in 150°F (65°C) oven. Repeat with remaining butter and batter. *(Pancakes can be covered and refrigerated for up to 1 day. To reheat, bake in single layer on baking sheet in 400°F/200°C oven for 4 to 5 minutes or until heated through.)* Makes about 60 pancakes.

# Golden Caviar and Eggs with Homemade Melba Toast

*Golden caviar is the roe from northern Manitoba whitefish and is available in refrigerated cans at specialty shops. Red lumpfish caviar can be substituted.*

| | | |
|---|---|---|
| 12 | hard-cooked eggs, coarsely chopped | 12 |
| 3/4 cup | (approx) mayonnaise | 175 mL |
| 1/4 cup | finely chopped green onion | 50 mL |
| 1 tsp | salt | 5 mL |
| 1/4 tsp | pepper | 1 mL |
| 1/4 tsp | dry mustard | 1 mL |
| 2 | jars (each 1.75 oz/50 g) whitefish caviar | 2 |
| 1 cup | sour cream | 250 mL |
| 15 | thin slices homemade-style white bread | 15 |
| 1/3 cup | finely chopped fresh parsley | 75 mL |

■ In bowl, combine eggs, mayonnaise, onion, salt, pepper and mustard, adding more mayonnaise if desired. Spoon into glass bowl, smoothing top. Spread with caviar, then sour cream. *(Spread can be covered and refrigerated for up to 1 day.)*

■ Remove crusts from bread; cut slices into triangles. Spread on baking sheets and toast in 250°F (120°C) oven until crisp and golden.

■ To serve, sprinkle parsley in ring around edge of bowl. Serve with toast. Makes 10 servings.

# Crunchy Parmesan Chicken Wings

*These Parmesan-coated wings make a satisfying snack.*

| | | |
|---|---|---|
| 4 lb | chicken wings | 2 kg |
| 1/2 cup | all-purpose flour | 125 mL |
| 1/2 tsp | paprika | 2 mL |
| 1/4 tsp | each salt and pepper | 1 mL |
| 4 | eggs | 4 |
| 2 cups | freshly grated Parmesan cheese | 500 mL |
| 1/2 cup | dry bread crumbs | 125 mL |
| 1 tsp | each dried basil and oregano | 5 mL |

■ Remove tips from chicken wings and reserve for stock if desired; separate wings at joints.

■ In shallow dish, combine flour, paprika, salt and pepper. In another shallow dish, beat eggs. In third shallow dish, combine cheese, bread crumbs, basil and oregano. Dip wings into flour mixture, then into eggs, then into cheese mixture, pressing firmly. *(Wings can be prepared to this point, placed on rack, covered and refrigerated for up to 4 hours.)*

■ Arrange wings on greased rimmed baking sheets. Bake in 375°F (190°C) oven for 35 to 40 minutes, turning once, or until golden brown and crisp. Makes about 60 pieces.

# Melon Soup

*This novel soup, made from a single melon, makes a fashionable starter for everything from casual cookouts to special dinners.*

| | | |
|---|---|---|
| 1 | cantaloupe | 1 |
| 1 | orange | 1 |
| 1/2 cup | whipping cream | 125 mL |
| 1 tsp | granulated sugar | 5 mL |
| Pinch | each salt and ginger | Pinch |

■ Quarter melon; remove seeds and outer rind. Cut melon into small pieces. In blender or food processor, process melon until smooth; transfer to bowl.

■ Grate rind from orange; reserve for garnish. Squeeze juice from orange; add to bowl along with cream, sugar, salt and ginger. Cover and refrigerate for at least 4 hours or until chilled. Sprinkle with orange rind. Makes 4 to 6 servings.

# Marinated Mussels

*Coriander and lime juice make a delicious marinade for mussels.*

| | | |
|---|---|---|
| 2 tbsp | chopped fresh coriander or parsley | 25 mL |
| 2 tbsp | olive oil | 25 mL |
| 2 tsp | lime juice | 10 mL |
| 1/4 tsp | pepper | 1 mL |
| 1/4 tsp | hot pepper sauce | 1 mL |
| 1 lb | mussels (about 24) | 500 g |
| 1 tbsp | chopped sweet red pepper | 15 mL |

■ In bowl, combine coriander, oil, lime juice, pepper and hot pepper sauce; taste and adjust seasoning if desired.

■ Scrub mussels and remove any beards; discard any that do not close when tapped. In large saucepan over medium heat, cook mussels in 1/4 cup (50 mL) water, covered, for about 4 minutes or until mussels open. Discard any that do not open.

■ Remove mussels from shells, reserving half the shells for serving. Transfer mussels to shallow bowl; pour marinade over mussels. Cover and marinate in refrigerator for up to 30 minutes. Arrange shells on serving platter; place one mussel on each shell. Garnish with red pepper. Makes about 24 appetizers.

*(on large plate) Marinated Mussels; Cucumber Slices with Shrimp and Chives (p. 12); Roasted Red Pepper and Cheese Bites (p. 13); Stuffed Cherry Tomatoes (p. 13); Pork Satays with Plum Sauce (p. 14); (on small plate) New Potatoes with Smoked Salmon (p. 12); Endive Spears (p. 14)* ►

# New Potatoes with Smoked Salmon

*These delicious new potatoes make an attractive addition to your buffet table. For an interesting variation, substitute smoked trout for the salmon.*

| | | |
|---|---|---|
| 24 | tiny red new potatoes (unpeeled), about 1-1/2 lb (750 g) | 24 |
| 1/4 cup | cream cheese | 50 mL |
| 1/4 cup | sour cream | 50 mL |
| 4 tsp | chopped fresh dill | 20 mL |
| Pinch | each salt and pepper | Pinch |
| 1-1/2 oz | smoked salmon, cut in thin strips | 45 g |
| 24 | dill sprigs or capers | 24 |

■ In pot of boiling water, cook potatoes for 16 to 20 minutes or until tender; let cool. Scoop out small spoonful of pulp from centre of each potato.

■ In bowl, combine cream cheese, sour cream, dill, salt and pepper; spoon about 1 tsp (5 mL) into each potato. Cover and refrigerate for at least 1 hour or up to 8 hours. To serve, top each potato with strip oɪ smoked salmon and dill sprig. Makes 24 appetizers.

# Cucumber Slices with Shrimp and Chives

*For a pretty decorative touch, garnish these appetizers with chive blossoms, as we did for the photograph (see page 11).*

| | | |
|---|---|---|
| 1 | seedless cucumber | 1 |
| 1/2 tsp | salt | 2 mL |
| 1 | pkg (5 oz/142 g) herb cream cheese, softened | 1 |
| 24 | small cooked shrimp | 24 |
| | Chives | |

■ Draw tines of fork lengthwise along cucumber to score; cut into 1/4-inch (5 mm) thick slices. Scoop out small amount of pulp from centre of each slice. Sprinkle slices with salt; drain on paper towel for 1 hour. Pat dry.

■ Using 1/4-inch (5 mm) open star tip, pipe or spoon about 1 tsp (5 mL) herb cream cheese onto each cucumber slice. Top with shrimp and chives. Makes 24 appetizers.

# Roasted Red Pepper and Cheese Bites

*The smoky flavor of roasted sweet red peppers and the mellow taste of mild mozzarella cheese make a great flavor combination in these appetizers.*

| | | |
|---|---|---|
| 2 | sweet red peppers | 2 |
| 1 tbsp | olive oil | 15 mL |
| 1/2 tsp | crushed black peppercorns | 2 mL |
| 3 oz | mozzarella or Asiago cheese, cut in 1/2-inch (1 cm) cubes | 90 g |

■ Broil peppers 4 to 6 inches (10 to 15 cm) from heat, turning often, for 15 to 20 minutes or until charred. Let cool slightly. Peel and seed; cut pepper lengthwise into 1/2-inch (1 cm) wide strips. Place in bowl and toss with oil and pepper.

■ Wrap 1 pepper strip around each cheese cube and secure with toothpick. Serve immediately. *(Cheese bites can be covered and refrigerated for up to 8 hours. Let come to room temperature before serving.)* Makes about 24 appetizers.

# Stuffed Cherry Tomatoes

*With a pastry bag, you can make appetizers that look as if they were prepared by a professional chef. But even without one, you can easily stuff these cherry tomatoes using a small coffee spoon.*

| | | |
|---|---|---|
| 3/4 cup | ricotta or cream cheese | 175 mL |
| 1/3 cup | chopped fresh basil or parsley | 75 mL |
| 4 tsp | olive oil | 20 mL |
| 1 | clove garlic, minced | 1 |
| 1/4 tsp | salt | 1 mL |
| Pinch | pepper | Pinch |
| 24 | cherry tomatoes | 24 |

■ In bowl, beat cheese by hand until creamy; beat in basil, oil, garlic, salt and pepper. Spoon into pastry bag fitted with 1/2-inch (1 cm) open star tip.

■ Using sharp or serrated knife, make "X" in bottom of each cherry tomato; scoop out seeds. Pipe cheese mixture into tomatoes. *(Appetizers can be covered and refrigerated for up to 8 hours.)* Makes 24 appetizers.

# Pork Satays with Plum Sauce

*If using wooden skewers, soak them in water for at least 30 minutes before using to prevent scorching. It's easier to slice the pork thinly if it's partly frozen.*

| | | |
|---|---|---|
| 2 lb | lean boneless pork loin | 1 kg |
| 2/3 cup | plum sauce | 150 mL |
| 2 tbsp | soy sauce | 25 mL |
| 1 tbsp | vegetable oil | 15 mL |
| 1/4 tsp | ginger | 1 mL |
| 1/4 tsp | dry mustard | 1 mL |

■ Trim pork; slice lengthwise into 1/4-inch (5 mm) thick slices; cut into 1-inch (2.5 cm) strips. Thread strips onto skewers; place on tray or platter.

■ Combine 1/3 cup (75 mL) of the plum sauce, soy sauce, oil, ginger and mustard; brush some of the mixture generously over meat. Cover and refrigerate for 1 hour.

■ Place skewers on greased grill over medium-hot coals or at medium setting; grill for 8 to 12 minutes or until no longer pink inside, turning halfway through and basting occasionally with sauce. Brush with remaining plum sauce just before serving. Makes about 24 appetizers.

# Endive Spears

*If Belgian endive isn't available, you can use leaves from two heads of radicchio or small leaves from the hearts of romaine lettuce.*

| | | |
|---|---|---|
| 1/4 cup | mayonnaise | 50 mL |
| 2 tbsp | sour cream | 25 mL |
| 24 | Belgian endive leaves (about 2 heads) | 24 |
| 24 | cooked shrimp | 24 |
| | Dill sprigs | |

■ In small bowl, combine mayonnaise and sour cream; spoon about 1/2 tsp (2 mL) onto each endive leaf. Top each with shrimp and dill sprig. Makes 24 appetizers.

# Green Bean Soup Amandine

*Green beans and almonds team up happily in this fresh-tasting soup. For very smooth results, use a blender to purée the soup.*

| | | |
|---|---|---|
| 1 lb | green beans, trimmed | 500 g |
| 2 tbsp | butter | 25 mL |
| 1/2 cup | ground almonds | 125 mL |
| 4 cups | chicken stock | 1 L |
| 1 | onion, chopped | 1 |
| 2 | cloves garlic, minced | 2 |
| 2 tsp | each finely chopped fresh rosemary and marjoram (or 1/2 tsp/2 mL each dried) | 10 mL |
| | Salt and white pepper | |
| 1/2 cup | whipping cream | 125 mL |
| | Sliced almonds | |

■ Cut beans into 1-1/2-inch (4 cm) pieces to make about 3 cups (750 mL); set aside.

■ In large saucepan, melt butter over medium heat; cook ground almonds, stirring, for 3 minutes or until golden. Add beans and 2 cups (500 mL) of the stock, onion, garlic, rosemary, marjoram, and salt and pepper to taste; bring to boil. Reduce heat and simmer, covered, for 8 to 10 minutes or until beans are tender.

■ In blender or food processor, purée soup in batches until smooth. Transfer to bowl; stir in remaining stock and cream. Cover and refrigerate until very cold, at least 4 hours or overnight.

■ Just before serving, taste and adjust seasoning if necessary. Ladle into chilled bowls; garnish with sliced almonds. Makes 4 to 6 servings.

# Broccoli Soup

*This broccoli soup is enhanced with the flavors of carrot, onion and garlic. It's also delicious served hot.*

| | | |
|---|---|---|
| 3 tbsp | butter | 50 mL |
| 1 | onion, sliced | 1 |
| 1 | carrot, sliced | 1 |
| 1 | clove garlic, minced | 1 |
| 4 cups | chicken stock | 1 L |
| 1 lb | broccoli, chopped | 500 g |
| 1 cup | light cream | 250 mL |
| | Salt and pepper | |
| | Chopped fresh parsley | |

■ In saucepan, melt butter over medium heat; cook onion, carrot and garlic for 5 minutes. Stir in stock and bring to boil; add broccoli. Reduce heat and simmer, covered, until broccoli is tender, 15 to 20 minutes.

■ In blender or food processor, purée soup in batches and transfer to glass bowl. Stir in cream; season with salt and pepper to taste. Cover and refrigerate for at least 4 hours or until chilled. Sprinkle with parsley just before serving. Makes 6 servings.

# Oriental Meatballs

*These tasty little meatballs can be cooled, covered and refrigerated for up to 1 day, or frozen for up to 2 weeks. Microwave at High for 1 to 3 minutes or until heated through.*

| | | |
|---|---|---|
| 1/2 lb | lean ground pork | 250 g |
| 2 | green onions (white and green parts), finely chopped | 2 |
| 1 | clove garlic, finely chopped | 1 |
| 2 tbsp | hoisin sauce | 25 mL |
| 1 tsp | cornstarch | 5 mL |
| 1 tsp | rice wine or sherry | 5 mL |
| 1/2 tsp | salt | 2 mL |
| | Sesame seeds (optional) | |
| | **SAUCE** | |
| 1/4 cup | smooth mango chutney | 50 mL |
| 1 tsp | hoisin sauce | 5 mL |

■ **Sauce:** In small bowl, stir chutney with hoisin sauce until well blended; set aside.

■ In bowl, combine pork, onions, garlic, hoisin sauce, cornstarch, rice wine and salt; mix thoroughly. Form into 1-inch (2.5 cm) balls and skewer on wooden toothpicks. Sprinkle with sesame seeds (if using).

■ Arrange meatballs in circle on microwaveable rack; microwave at High for 4 to 5 minutes or until no longer pink inside. Serve with sauce for dipping. Makes about 20 appetizers.

*(left to right) Lobster Spread on Belgian Endive; Oriental Meatballs; skewered cooked chicken and vegetables; Tiny Tuna Melts* ▲

# Tiny Tuna Melts

*Use packaged miniature toasts or prepare your own for this bite-size version of a familiar favorite.*

| | | |
|---|---|---|
| 1 | can (6.5 oz/184 g) tuna, drained | 1 |
| 1/3 cup | mayonnaise | 75 mL |
| 1/4 tsp | lemon juice | 1 mL |
| | Pepper | |
| 1 | pkg (36) miniature toasts (each 1-1/2 inches/4 cm square) or homemade crisps* | 1 |
| 1/4 lb | Swiss or Cheddar cheese, sliced | 125 g |
| 2 tbsp | chopped green onion, slivered sweet green pepper or green olives | 25 mL |

■ In bowl, combine tuna, mayonnaise, lemon juice, and pepper to taste; spread evenly over toasts. Top with slice of cheese; sprinkle with green onion.

■ Arrange half of the tuna toasts in circle on microwaveable plate; microwave at High for 30 to 60 seconds or just until cheese begins to melt. Repeat with remaining tuna toasts. Makes 36 appetizers.

*To make bread crisps, remove crusts from 9 slices of sandwich bread; cut each slice into 4 squares. Arrange half of the squares on microwaveable plate; microwave at High for 3 to 4 minutes or until crisp and dry. Repeat with remaining bread.

# Lobster Spread on Belgian Endive

*The exquisite flavors of lobster and caviar are enhanced by delicate Belgian endive.*

| | | |
|---|---|---|
| 2 | hard-cooked eggs | 2 |
| 3 tbsp | mayonnaise | 50 mL |
| 1 | can (2.5 oz/71 g) lobster, drained | 1 |
| 1/2 tsp | lemon juice | 2 mL |
| Pinch | cayenne pepper | Pinch |
| 3 | Belgian endives | 3 |
| | **GARNISH** | |
| | Red or black caviar | |

■ Remove egg yolks and finely chop; set whites aside. Combine yolks with 2 tsp (10 mL) of the mayonnaise; set aside. In blender or food processor, combine egg whites, lobster, lemon juice, cayenne pepper and remaining mayonnaise; blend until smooth. *(Recipe can be prepared to this point, covered and refrigerated for up to 1 day.)*

■ Separate Belgian endive leaves. Spoon 1 tsp (5 mL) lobster mixture onto stem end of each leaf. Top with 1/2 tsp (2 mL) egg yolk mixture. Garnish with sprinkle of caviar. Makes about 30 appetizers.

# Spinach Feta Ring

*An attractive and tasty dish, this is perfect for any brunch menu. Garnish platter with tomato wedges and spinach leaves and serve with toasted pita bread triangles.*

| | | |
|---|---|---|
| 6 cups | trimmed spinach | 1.5 L |
| 1 tbsp | butter | 15 mL |
| 1 | small onion, finely chopped | 1 |
| 3/4 cup | milk | 175 mL |
| 1/2 cup | crumbled feta cheese | 125 mL |
| 1/2 cup | fresh bread crumbs | 125 mL |
| 2 tbsp | chopped fresh dill | 25 mL |
| 2 tsp | grated lemon rind | 10 mL |
| 1/4 tsp | pepper | 1 mL |
| 3 | eggs, lightly beaten | 3 |
| | Lemon wedges | |

■ **Microwave method:** Wash spinach; shake off excess water. With just the water clinging to leaves, place spinach in 12-cup (3 L) microwaveable casserole; cover and microwave at High for 3 minutes or just until wilted, stirring once. Drain and line 4-cup (1 L) microwaveable greased ring mould with 8 to 10 large leaves; set aside. Squeeze excess moisture from remaining spinach; chop and set aside.

■ In 8-cup (2 L) microwaveable bowl, combine butter with onion; microwave at High for 2 minutes or until onion is softened, stirring once. Stir in milk, cheese, bread crumbs, dill, lemon rind, pepper, eggs and reserved chopped spinach; mix well.

■ Spoon into spinach-lined mould; microwave, uncovered, at Medium (50%) for 10 minutes or until slightly firm to the touch and knife inserted 1/2 inch (1 cm) from centre comes out clean, rotating ring mould twice. Let stand for 5 minutes. Invert onto serving platter; serve with lemon wedges.

■ **Conventional method:** Wash spinach; shake off excess water and place in saucepan. With just the water clinging to leaves, cook spinach, uncovered, for 3 to 5 minutes or just until wilted. Drain. Line 4-cup (1 L) greased ring mould with 8 to 10 leaves; set aside. Squeeze excess moisture from remaining spinach; chop and place in bowl.

■ Wipe out skillet and heat butter over medium heat; cook onion for 3 minutes or until softened. Add to spinach along with milk, cheese, bread crumbs, dill, lemon rind, pepper and eggs; mix well.

■ Pour into spinach-lined mould; bake in 350°F (180°C) oven for 25 to 30 minutes or until set. Invert onto serving platter; serve with lemon wedges.

■ Makes about 4 servings.

# Mustard Baked Chicken

*Serve this easy-to-make chicken dish with tender-crisp buttered asparagus and baby carrot chunks lightly seasoned with chopped fresh dill. Garnish with red-tipped leaf lettuce.*

| | | |
|---|---|---|
| 2-1/2 lb | chicken pieces | 1.25 kg |
| 1/3 cup | Dijon mustard | 75 mL |
| 1 tbsp | apricot jam | 15 mL |
| 1/2 cup | white wine or chicken stock | 125 mL |
| 3/4 cup | whipping cream | 175 mL |
| | Salt and pepper | |
| 2 tbsp | chopped fresh parsley | 25 mL |
| | Lemon slices | |

*ELEGANT CHICKEN DISHES*

*Chicken is a universal favorite, ideal for entertaining because it's so versatile and economical. It's compatible with a range of sauces and seasonings and lends itself to a variety of preparation and cooking methods.*

*• The key to an attractive entrée is the presentation. Add extra flair with colorful garnishes or vegetables. We've included several delicious recipes for chicken in this section.*

■ In lightly greased flameproof 13- × 9-inch (3.5 L) baking dish, arrange chicken pieces skin side down in single layer. Combine mustard and jam; brush half of the mixture over chicken.

■ Bake in 375°F (190°C) oven for 20 minutes. Turn chicken pieces over; brush with remaining mustard mixture. Bake for 20 minutes longer or until golden and juices run clear when chicken is pierced. Transfer to serving plate and keep warm.

■ Pour off excess fat from baking dish. Add wine; bring to boil over medium-high heat, stirring to scrape up any browned bits. Transfer to small saucepan; cook for 5 minutes or until reduced by half. Add cream and cook, stirring, for 4 to 5 minutes or until thick enough to coat back of spoon. Season with salt and pepper to taste. Pour over chicken; sprinkle with parsley. Garnish with lemon slices. Makes 4 or 5 servings.

# Chicken con Queso

*When preparing chicken and rice, cook extra to make this zippy casserole to store in the freezer for unexpected company.*

| | | |
|---|---|---|
| 1/4 cup | butter | 50 mL |
| 1 | onion, chopped | 1 |
| 2 | cloves garlic, minced | 2 |
| 1/4 cup | all-purpose flour | 50 mL |
| 3 cups | hot milk | 750 mL |
| 3 cups | shredded Cheddar or Monterey Jack cheese | 750 mL |
| 1/4 cup | each chopped fresh parsley and coriander | 50 mL |
| 2 tbsp | tomato paste | 25 mL |
| 1 tsp | chili powder | 5 mL |
| 1/2 tsp | dried oregano | 2 mL |
| 1 | can (4 oz/113 g) green chili peppers, drained and chopped | 1 |
| 3 | green onions, chopped | 3 |
| | Salt and pepper | |
| 2 cups | cooked rice | 500 mL |
| 2 cups | diced cooked chicken | 500 mL |
| 1 cup | coarsely crushed corn chips | 250 mL |

■ In large saucepan, melt butter over medium heat; cook onion and garlic, stirring, for 3 minutes or until softened. Add flour and cook, stirring, for 5 minutes. Whisk in milk; cook, stirring often, until sauce thickens, about 10 minutes. Remove from heat.

■ Add 2 cups (500 mL) of the cheese; stir until melted. Stir in parsley, coriander, tomato paste, chili powder, oregano, chili peppers, green onions, and salt and pepper to taste.

■ Spread half of the sauce in shallow 8-inch (2 L) square casserole; top with rice, then chicken. Cover with remaining sauce. *(Recipe can be prepared to this point, cooled, covered and refrigerated for up to 2 days or frozen for up to 3 months. Thaw before proceeding.)*

■ Bake, covered, in 400°F (200°C) oven for 30 minutes. Reduce heat to 375°F (190°C); bake for 10 minutes. Sprinkle on chips and remaining cheese; bake for 15 minutes or until bubbling and top is golden. (Or microwave at Medium-High/70% for 15 to 20 minutes or until heated through, rotating once. Sprinkle on chips and cheese; let stand, covered, for 10 minutes or until cheese has melted.) Makes 6 servings.

# Linguine with Scallops in Curried Cream Sauce

*Scallops are sweet, succulent and worth the treat. Nibble on a mild pâté appetizer and finish with a fresh fruit dessert.*

| | | |
|---|---|---|
| 1/4 cup | butter | 50 mL |
| 2 | cloves garlic, minced | 2 |
| 2 tsp | minced gingerroot | 10 mL |
| 1 tbsp | curry powder | 15 mL |
| 1 cup | whipping cream | 250 mL |
| 1 lb | scallops | 500 g |
| 1 | sweet red pepper, peeled, seeded and diced | 1 |
| 1/2 cup | dry white wine or chicken stock | 125 mL |
| 1 lb | linguine | 500 g |
| 1/4 cup | chopped green onions | 50 mL |
| | Salt and pepper | |

■ In skillet, melt half of the butter over medium heat, cook garlic and gingerroot for 2 minutes or until fragrant and tender but not browned.

■ Add curry powder; cook for 1 minute, stirring constantly. Pour in cream; increase heat to medium-high and bring to boil. Cook until sauce is reduced to about 3/4 cup (175 mL).

■ Meanwhile, cut scallops crosswise into 1/4-inch (5 mm) thick rounds; set aside. In separate skillet, melt remaining butter over medium-high heat, cook red pepper, stirring occasionally, for about 2 minutes or until softened slightly. Pour in wine; bring to boil. Reduce heat to low; add scallops. Cover and simmer for 2 to 3 minutes or until scallops are opaque.

■ With slotted spoon, remove scallops and red pepper; set aside. Increase heat to medium-high; cook liquid for 2 minutes or until reduced to 1/4 cup (50 mL). Stir into cream sauce along with scallops and red pepper.

■ Meanwhile, in large pot of boiling salted water, cook linguine until tender but firm; drain well. Toss with scallop mixture and onions. Season with salt and pepper to taste. Makes about 6 servings.

# Creole Shrimp and Fish with Rice

*This spicy layered casserole is a delicious make-ahead dish for a casual foursome.*
*The recipe can be doubled for a larger event, such as a buffet.*

| | | |
|---|---|---|
| 1 tbsp | butter | 15 mL |
| 1/2 cup | each chopped onion and sweet green pepper | 125 mL |
| 1/4 cup | chopped celery | 50 mL |
| 1 | clove garlic, minced | 1 |
| 1 | can (19 oz/540 mL) tomatoes (undrained) | 1 |
| 1 | bay leaf | 1 |
| 1/2 tsp | each dried basil and salt | 2 mL |
| 1/4 tsp | dried thyme | 1 mL |
| Pinch | hot pepper flakes and pepper | Pinch |
| 1/2 lb | deveined peeled shrimp | 250 g |
| 1/2 lb | haddock, cut in 2-inch (5 cm) cubes | 250 g |
| 1/2 cup | long-grain rice, cooked | 125 mL |
| 1 | green onion, sliced | 1 |

■ In large saucepan, melt butter over medium heat; cook onion, green pepper, celery and garlic for 5 minutes.

■ Stir in tomatoes, bay leaf, basil, salt, thyme, hot pepper flakes and pepper, crushing tomatoes with spoon; bring to boil. Reduce heat and simmer, stirring occasionally, for 7 minutes or until slightly thickened. Remove bay leaf.

■ Meanwhile, place shrimp in saucepan of lightly salted boiling water. Cover and remove from heat; let stand for 2 minutes. With slotted spoon, remove shrimp; set aside. Return water to boil. Add haddock and repeat.

■ Combine cooked rice with green onion. In greased 6-cup (1.5 L) casserole, layer half of the rice mixture, half of the shrimp, half of the fish and half of the sauce. Repeat with remaining ingredients. *(Recipe can be cooled, covered and refrigerated for up to 1 day.)* Bake, covered, in 325°F (160°C) oven for 45 to 50 minutes or until heated through. Makes 4 servings.

# Rosemary Lamb Chops

*Serve boiled new potatoes and sugar snap peas with these lemon- and rosemary-scented lamb chops. The recipe can be easily doubled for more servings.*

| | | |
|---|---|---|
| 2 tbsp | olive oil | 25 mL |
| 2 tsp | grated lemon rind | 10 mL |
| 4 tsp | lemon juice | 20 mL |
| 2 | cloves garlic, minced | 2 |
| 2 tsp | chopped fresh rosemary (or 1/2 tsp/2 mL dried) | 10 mL |
| 4 | lamb loin chops (about 1 lb/500 g total) | 4 |
| | Salt and pepper | |
| | Rosemary sprigs | |

■ Combine oil, lemon rind and juice, garlic and chopped rosemary. Place lamb in shallow dish; pour marinade over. Cover and refrigerate for up to 2 hours, turning occasionally. Remove from refrigerator 30 minutes before cooking. Remove chops from marinade.

■ Broil chops 4 inches (10 cm) from heat for 5 to 6 minutes per side or until still slightly pink inside. (Alternatively, pan-fry in lightly greased skillet over medium heat for 10 minutes per side.) Season with salt and pepper to taste. Garnish with rosemary sprigs. Makes 2 servings.

# Veal Rolls with Mushroom Sauce

*These veal rolls — with a savory stuffing and mushroom sauce — are reminiscent of mock duck, which was often made with thin slices of flank or round steak.*

| | | |
|---|---|---|
| 1/3 lb | ground pork | 175 g |
| 1/4 cup | finely chopped onion | 50 mL |
| 1 | clove garlic, minced | 1 |
| 1/4 cup | finely chopped celery | 50 mL |
| 1/2 tsp | dried sage | 2 mL |
| 1/4 tsp | pepper | 1 mL |
| Pinch | cloves | Pinch |
| 3/4 cup | fresh whole wheat bread crumbs | 175 mL |
| 3 tbsp | beef stock or water | 50 mL |
| 4 | thin veal cutlets (about 1/2 lb/250 g total) | 4 |
| | All-purpose flour | |

| MUSHROOM SAUCE | | |
|---|---|---|
| 1 tbsp | vegetable oil | 15 mL |
| 1 | clove garlic, halved | 1 |
| 1/2 lb | mushrooms, thinly sliced | 250 g |
| 1 cup | beef stock | 250 mL |
| 1/4 cup | dry red wine | 50 mL |
| 1/4 tsp | pepper | 1 mL |
| Pinch | dried sage | Pinch |
| 1 tbsp | all-purpose flour | 15 mL |
| 1 tbsp | butter, softened | 15 mL |
| 2 tbsp | whipping cream (optional) | 25 mL |

■ In skillet, combine pork, onion, garlic, celery, sage, pepper and cloves; cook over medium heat, breaking up meat with back of spoon, for about 5 minutes or until pork is no longer pink. Drain off excess fat if necessary. Stir in bread crumbs and stock. Remove from heat; let stand for 5 minutes.

■ Divide stuffing among cutlets, spreading evenly and leaving 1/2-inch (1 cm) border at narrow end of each cutlet. Beginning at wide end, roll up jelly-roll style; secure with toothpicks or string. Lightly dredge rolls with flour.

■ **Mushroom Sauce:** In skillet, heat oil over medium-high heat; cook garlic, stirring, for 1 minute, then discard. Add veal rolls; cook for about 7 minutes or until browned on all sides. Transfer to 8-inch (2 L) square baking dish; remove toothpicks. Set aside.

■ Add mushrooms to skillet; cook over medium-high heat for 3 to 4 minutes or just until softened. Stir in stock, wine, pepper and sage; bring to boil. Cook over medium-high heat for about 4 minutes or until reduced slightly. Blend flour with butter to make smooth paste; stir into mushroom mixture until smooth. Cook, stirring, for 1 to 2 minutes or until thickened.

■ Pour sauce over veal rolls. Cover and bake in 350°F (180°C) oven for 35 to 45 minutes or until tender and heated through. *(Recipe can be prepared to this point, cooled, covered and refrigerated for up to 24 hours. To reheat, bake in 350°F/180°C oven for 30 minutes or until heated through.)*

■ With slotted spoon, transfer rolls to serving plate. Stir cream (if using) into sauce and spoon over rolls. Makes 4 servings.

# Stir-Fried Chicken with Rice Noodles

*Rice or bean thread noodles need only to be soaked before using.*

| | | |
|---|---|---|
| 1/4 lb | wide rice-stick or bean thread noodles | 125 g |
| 2 tsp | vegetable oil | 10 mL |
| 2 | cloves garlic, minced | 2 |
| 1 tbsp | minced gingerroot | 15 mL |
| 3 | green onions, chopped | 3 |
| 1 lb | boneless skinless chicken breasts, cut in 1-inch (2.5 cm) pieces | 500 g |
| 1 | sweet red pepper, cut in 1-inch (2.5 cm) pieces | 1 |
| 4 | carrots, thinly sliced on diagonal | 4 |
| 6 cups | broccoli pieces | 1.5 L |
| 1-1/2 cups | chicken stock | 375 mL |
| 1/4 lb | snow peas, trimmed | 125 g |
| | Salt and pepper | |

| SAUCE | | |
|---|---|---|
| 2 tbsp | cornstarch | 25 mL |
| 2 tbsp | soy sauce | 25 mL |
| 2 tbsp | hoisin sauce | 25 mL |
| 2 tsp | sesame oil | 10 mL |
| 1/4 tsp | (approx) hot chili paste or hot pepper sauce (optional) | 1 mL |

■ Break up noodles and place in bowl; cover with boiling water and let stand for 5 to 10 minutes or until softened. Drain well.

■ Meanwhile, in wok or large heavy nonstick pan, heat oil over medium-high heat; stir-fry garlic, gingerroot and green onions for 30 seconds or until fragrant. Add chicken; stir-fry for 2 minutes. Stir in red pepper, carrots and broccoli. Add stock; cover and cook for 3 to 4 minutes or until vegetables are tender-crisp.

■ **Sauce:** Combine cornstarch, soy sauce, hoisin sauce, sesame oil, and chili paste (if using).

■ Stir snow peas and noodles into chicken mixture; bring to boil. Stir in sauce and cook for 1 minute or until sauce is thickened and glossy. Season with salt, pepper and more chili paste to taste. Makes 4 servings.

# *Paella*

*Done peasant-style with chicken and sausages, paella is gentle on the pocketbook; made with scallops and shrimp, it's a king's treat. You can substitute 2 cans (each 28 oz/796 mL) plum tomatoes, drained, seeded and chopped, for the fresh tomatoes.*

| | | | | | | |
|---|---|---|---|---|---|---|
| 1 | chicken (about 3 lb/1.5 kg) | 1 | 1/2 lb | shrimp, peeled and deveined | 250 g |
| 1/2 cup | all-purpose flour | 125 mL | 1/2 lb | scallops | 250 g |
| | Salt and pepper | | 1/2 lb | mussels, cleaned | 250 g |
| 3 tbsp | olive oil | 50 mL | 3 tbsp | chopped chives or green onions | 50 mL |
| 1 | onion, coarsely chopped | 1 | | | |
| 2 | cloves garlic, finely chopped | 2 | | | |
| 3 | large tomatoes, peeled, seeded and diced | 3 | | | |
| 2 | sweet red peppers, cut in large chunks | 2 | | | |
| 1-1/2 cups | short- or long-grain rice | 375 mL | | | |
| 1/2 tsp | saffron threads (or 1/4 tsp/1 mL powder) | 2 mL | | | |
| 3 cups | hot chicken stock | 750 mL | | | |

■ Cut chicken into 10 pieces. Dredge in flour; season with salt and pepper to taste.

■ In large deep skillet or Dutch oven, heat oil over medium-high heat; cook chicken, in batches, for 5 to 10 minutes or until browned. Remove from skillet and set aside.

■ Discard all but about 3 tbsp (50 mL) fat from skillet. Cook onion with garlic over medium-high heat for about 3 minutes or until tender. Add tomatoes and red peppers; cook for 5 minutes or until softened. Add rice, stirring to coat well.

■ Dissolve saffron in stock; stir into rice mixture. Bring to boil; reduce heat to low. Return chicken to skillet; cover and simmer gently for 40 minutes.

■ Arrange shrimp, scallops and mussels in rice mixture; cover and cook for 10 to 15 minutes or until rice is tender, mussels have opened (discard any that haven't), scallops are opaque, shrimp are pink and chicken is no longer pink inside. Season with salt and pepper to taste. Sprinkle with chives. Makes 6 to 8 servings.

# Sautéed Pork with Red Pepper Sauce

*For an equally tasty but cheaper alternative to pork tenderloin, cut well-trimmed*
*1-inch (2.5 cm) thick boneless loin pork chops diagonally into 1/4-inch (5 mm) thick*
*slices. You can toss the red pepper sauce with pasta, too, if desired.*

| | | |
|---|---|---|
| 1 lb | pork tenderloin | 500 g |
| 3 tbsp | all-purpose flour | 50 mL |
| 3 tbsp | (approx) vegetable oil | 50 mL |
| 1 | large sweet red pepper, sliced | 1 |
| 1 | clove garlic, minced | 1 |
| 1-1/2 tsp | chopped fresh basil (or 1/2 tsp/2 mL dried) | 7 mL |
| 1 cup | low-fat ricotta cheese | 250 mL |
| 1 tbsp | Dijon mustard | 15 mL |
| 1 cup | chicken stock | 250 mL |

■ Cut pork diagonally across the grain into 1/4-inch (5 mm) thick slices. Coat with flour, shaking off excess.

■ In large skillet, heat 1 tbsp (15 mL) of the oil over medium heat; cook red pepper, garlic and basil for 3 minutes. With slotted spoon, transfer to food processor or blender; purée. Add cheese and mustard; process until well blended.

■ Add 1 tbsp (15 mL) of the oil to skillet; cook pork over medium-high heat, in batches and adding more oil if necessary, for 4 to 5 minutes or until browned outside and no longer pink inside. Transfer to serving platter; keep warm.

■ Add stock to skillet; bring to boil, scraping up any browned bits on bottom of pan. Whisk in red pepper mixture and heat through. Pour some sauce over pork. Pass remaining sauce separately. Makes 4 servings.

> *DINNER IN 30 MINUTES*
> *Here's a menu that's perfect for unexpected weekday dinner guests. Accompany Sautéed Pork with Red Pepper Sauce (this page) with Garlicky Broccoli Pasta (p. 41) and a simple tossed salad. End the meal with a refreshing dessert of blueberries with lemon sherbet.*

# Moussaka for a Crowd

*This is the ultimate make-ahead casserole, robust and flavorful, and will get raves, even from avowed eggplant haters.*

| | | |
|---|---|---|
| 2 | large eggplants | 2 |
| 1 tsp | salt | 5 mL |
| 1/4 cup | olive oil | 50 mL |
| 3 cups | chopped onions | 750 mL |
| 2 lb | lean ground beef | 1 kg |
| 1/2 cup | dry red wine or beef stock | 125 mL |
| 1/4 cup | tomato paste | 50 mL |
| 1/2 tsp | cinnamon | 2 mL |
| 1/4 tsp | pepper | 1 mL |
| 1/2 cup | minced fresh parsley | 125 mL |
| 1 cup | fresh bread crumbs | 250 mL |
| 1 cup | freshly grated Parmesan cheese | 250 mL |
| 1/4 cup | butter | 50 mL |
| 1/3 cup | all-purpose flour | 75 mL |
| 4 cups | milk | 1 L |
| 4 | eggs, lightly beaten | 4 |
| 2 cups | creamed cottage cheese | 500 mL |
| 1 tsp | nutmeg | 5 mL |

■ Trim eggplants; cut lengthwise into 1/2-inch (1 cm) thick slices. In colander, layer slices with salt; let stand for 30 minutes. Rinse and pat dry.

■ In large nonstick skillet, heat 1 tbsp (15 mL) of the oil over medium-high heat; brown eggplant in batches, adding a little more oil as necessary; remove and set aside.

■ Pour remaining oil into skillet; cook onions over medium heat until softened, about 5 minutes. Add beef and increase heat to high; cook, stirring to break up meat, until no longer pink. Add wine, tomato paste, cinnamon and pepper; bring to boil. Reduce heat and simmer for about 10 minutes or until thickened; stir in parsley. Taste and adjust seasoning; set aside.

■ Sprinkle 13- × 9-inch (3.5 L) baking dish lightly with some of the bread crumbs. Cover with half of the eggplant, meat sauce, bread crumbs and Parmesan cheese. Repeat with remaining eggplant, meat sauce, bread crumbs and Parmesan. *(Recipe can be prepared to this point and frozen. Thaw before continuing.)*

■ In heavy saucepan, melt butter over medium heat; cook flour, stirring, for about 3 minutes without browning. Gradually whisk in milk to make smooth sauce; let cool slightly. Stir in eggs, cottage cheese and nutmeg; spoon over eggplant mixture. *(Recipe can be prepared to this point, cooled, covered and refrigerated for up to 1 day.)*

■ Bake in 375°F (190°C) oven for about 1 hour or until top is golden and moussaka is heated through and bubbling. Let stand for about 10 minutes before cutting into squares. Makes 8 to 10 servings.

# Thai Thighs

*Peanut butter adds a Thai touch to budget-priced chicken legs or thighs.*

| | | |
|---|---|---|
| 1/3 cup | minced green onions | 75 mL |
| 2 | cloves garlic, minced | 2 |
| 3 tbsp | hoisin sauce | 50 mL |
| 2 tbsp | peanut butter | 25 mL |
| 1 tbsp | minced gingerroot | 15 mL |
| 1 tbsp | soy sauce | 15 mL |
| 1 tbsp | sesame oil | 15 mL |
| 1 tbsp | lemon juice | 15 mL |
| 1/2 tsp | hot pepper sauce | 2 mL |
| 2 lb | chicken legs or thighs | 1 kg |
| 2 tbsp | chopped fresh coriander or parsley | 25 mL |

■ In bowl, combine 1/4 cup (50 mL) of the onions, garlic, hoisin sauce, peanut butter, gingerroot, soy sauce, sesame oil, lemon juice and hot pepper sauce.

■ Arrange chicken in shallow baking dish. Spoon sauce over chicken; bake in 375°F (190°C) oven for 45 to 50 minutes or until golden brown and juices run clear when chicken is pierced with fork. Sprinkle with remaining green onion and coriander. Makes 4 servings.

# Microwave Pork Roast with Apples

*Use apples that keep their shape after cooking, such as Northern Spy, Golden Delicious or Idared. Garnish the platter with fresh parsley.*

| | | |
|---|---|---|
| 3 lb | **boneless pork shoulder roast** | 1.5 kg |
| 2 cups | **sliced onions** | 500 mL |
| 1 tbsp | **butter** | 15 mL |
| 3 | **apples, peeled and thickly sliced** | 3 |
| 1 tsp | **dried thyme** | 5 mL |
| | **Salt and pepper** | |

*MICROWAVE POWER COOKING*

*Many newcomers to the microwave world think mainly of fast cooking and use only the High power setting. But just as you use different temperatures in a conventional oven for roasts, meringues and apple pies, you need different power levels when microwaving various foods. The recipes on these two pages use various power levels for succulent results.*

■ Trim excess fat from pork. In deep 12-cup (3 L) microwaveable casserole, microwave onions and butter at High for 4 minutes or until softened, stirring once. Scatter apples over top; nestle roast in apples. Sprinkle with thyme.

■ Cover and microwave at High for 5 minutes. Microwave at Medium (50%) for 1 hour or until thermometer registers 160 to 170°F (71 to 75°F), turning roast over halfway through and rotating dish twice.

■ Let stand, covered, for 10 minutes. Season with salt and pepper to taste. Slice meat and arrange on platter; surround with apple mixture. Makes about 8 servings.

# Microwave Marinated Brisket

*Tender enough to cut with a fork, this sweet-sour meat is great with noodles.*

| | | |
|---|---|---|
| 3 lb | beef brisket | 1.5 kg |
| 2 tsp | paprika | 10 mL |
| 1 tsp | dry mustard | 5 mL |
| 1/2 tsp | pepper | 2 mL |
| 2 | onions, chopped | 2 |
| 1/2 cup | orange juice | 125 mL |
| 1/3 cup | soy sauce | 75 mL |
| 3 tbsp | liquid honey | 50 mL |
| 2 | cloves garlic, minced | 2 |

■ Trim excess fat from meat. Combine paprika, mustard and pepper; rub over meat. Spread onions in 12-cup (3 L) shallow microwaveable casserole; top with brisket. Combine orange juice, soy sauce, honey and garlic; pour over meat and turn to coat. Cover and refrigerate to marinate overnight. Let stand at room temperature for 30 minutes.

■ Microwave, covered, at High for 5 minutes; turn meat over. Microwave, covered, at Medium (50%) for 90 minutes, basting occasionally, turning meat over halfway through and rotating dish twice. Let stand, covered, for 20 minutes.

■ Slice meat across the grain; return to casserole. Microwave, covered, at Medium (50%) for 30 to 40 minutes or until fork-tender. Makes about 8 servings.

# Stuffed Chicken Breasts

*Stuffed chicken breasts are elegant entertaining fare. Boneless breasts are fine, too, as long as they have a good covering of skin.*

| | | |
|---|---|---|
| 8 | chicken breasts | 8 |
| 2 tbsp | butter, melted | 25 mL |
| | **STUFFING** | |
| 2 tbsp | butter | 25 mL |
| 2 | green onions, minced | 2 |
| 3/4 cup | parboiled rice | 175 mL |
| 1/2 cup | currants | 125 mL |
| 1/4 cup | chopped dried apricots | 50 mL |
| 1-3/4 cups | chicken stock | 425 mL |
| 1 tsp | grated orange rind | 5 mL |
| 1/4 cup | orange juice | 50 mL |
| 1/4 cup | toasted slivered almonds or pine nuts | 50 mL |
| | Salt and pepper | |
| 2 oz | cream cheese, cubed | 50 g |

■ **Stuffing:** In heavy saucepan, melt butter over medium heat; cook onions, stirring, for about 1 minute or until softened. Add rice, currants and apricots, stirring to coat.

■ Add stock, orange rind and juice; bring to boil over high heat. Reduce heat and simmer, covered, for 15 to 20 minutes or until rice is tender and moisture is absorbed. Add almonds, and salt and pepper to taste. Fold in cream cheese; let cool completely.

■ Meanwhile, using sharp knife, remove bones from chicken breasts, leaving skin intact. Gently loosen skin from 1 long side of each breast, leaving skin attached along curved edge. Stuff about 1/2 cup (125 mL) stuffing under skin, pressing to spread stuffing evenly. Tuck ends of skin and meat underneath.

■ Place chicken on greased rimmed baking sheet; brush with butter. Bake in 375°F (190°C) oven, basting occasionally, for about 35 minutes or until golden brown and chicken is no longer pink inside. Skim fat from pan juices and serve pan juices with chicken. Makes 8 servings.

# Seafood and Broccoli Lasagna

*An elegant lasagna makes a delicious focal point for a brunch or supper buffet. Accompany with crusty brown rolls and a salad of Boston lettuce and cherry tomatoes.*

| | | |
|---|---|---|
| 6 | lasagna noodles | 6 |
| 1 lb | sole fillets | 500 g |
| 3 cups | milk | 750 mL |
| 1 lb | broccoli | 500 g |
| 1/3 cup | butter | 75 mL |
| 1/2 lb | mushrooms, sliced | 250 g |
| 1/3 cup | all-purpose flour | 75 mL |
| 1/2 tsp | salt | 2 mL |
| Pinch | each pepper and nutmeg | Pinch |
| 1/4 cup | whipping cream | 50 mL |
| 2-1/4 cups | shredded Swiss or mozzarella cheese | 550 mL |
| 3/4 lb | cooked shrimp | 375 g |
| 1/2 cup | freshly grated Parmesan cheese | 125 mL |

■ In large pot of boiling salted water, cook lasagna until tender but firm; drain and refresh with cold water. Set aside on paper towels.

■ In shallow saucepan, bring sole and milk to simmer; cook, covered, for 5 minutes or until fish flakes easily when tested with fork. Drain well, reserving hot milk.

■ Meanwhile, peel and slice broccoli stalks; divide florets into bite-size pieces. In large pot of boiling salted water, cook broccoli for 2 minutes; drain and refresh under cold water. Drain well and set aside on paper towels.

■ In saucepan, melt butter over medium heat; cook mushrooms for 3 to 5 minutes or until softened. Add flour; cook, stirring, over low heat for 2 minutes without browning. Remove from heat. Stir in reserved hot milk, salt, pepper and nutmeg; cook over medium heat, stirring, until thickened. Reduce heat to low; gradually stir in cream. Remove from heat. Taste and adjust seasoning. Stir in 1 cup (250 mL) of the Swiss cheese. Lightly spread some of the sauce in greased 13- × 9-inch (3 L) glass baking dish.

■ Flake sole; stir sole and shrimp into sauce in pan. Arrange 3 lasagna noodles in dish; spoon thin layer of sauce over top, spreading carefully to cover noodles. Arrange broccoli on top, dot with a few tablespoons of sauce.

■ Stir 1/4 cup (125 mL) of the Parmesan into remaining Swiss cheese; sprinkle half over broccoli. Top with 3 more noodles; top with remaining sauce. Sprinkle with remaining cheese mixture; top with remaining Parmesan. *(Recipe can be prepared to this point, covered and refrigerated for up to 8 hours.)*

■ Cover with foil; bake in 350°F (180°C) oven for 30 minutes. Uncover and broil for about 2 minutes or until golden brown on top. Makes 6 to 8 servings.

# Stuffed Zucchini

*Chopped zucchini mixed with bread crumbs and zingy fresh herbs is both refreshing and tasty when served in zucchini boats on a pool of fragrant tomato salsa.*

| | | |
|---|---|---|
| 6 | small zucchini (about 1-1/3 lb/675 g total) | 6 |
| 2 tbsp | olive oil | 25 mL |
| 3 tbsp | chopped fresh parsley | 50 mL |
| 2 tbsp | chopped fresh basil | 25 mL |
| 1 | clove garlic, minced | 1 |
| 1-1/2 cups | fresh bread crumbs | 375 mL |
| 1 | egg, beaten | 1 |
| | Salt and pepper | |
| 1/2 cup | chicken stock | 125 mL |
| | Chervil or parsley sprigs | |

| TOMATO SALSA | | |
|---|---|---|
| 1 lb | tomatoes (2 large) | 500 g |
| 3 tbsp | chopped fresh basil | 50 mL |
| 3 tbsp | olive oil | 50 mL |
| 1 tbsp | chopped fresh chervil or parsley | 15 mL |
| 1 tsp | each grated orange and lemon rind | 5 mL |
| 1 | clove garlic, minced | 1 |
| | Salt and pepper | |

■ **Tomato Salsa:** Peel, seed and chop tomatoes. In bowl, combine tomatoes, basil, oil, chervil, orange and lemon rind and garlic; season with salt and pepper to taste. Set aside for up to 1 hour at room temperature or cover and refrigerate for up to 2 days.

■ Cut off stem ends of zucchini. Cut off thin slice lengthwise on top. If necessary, trim bottoms so shells stand evenly. Reserve trimmings. Using grapefruit spoon or melon baller, scoop out zucchini flesh, leaving 1/4-inch (5 mm) thick shells. Chop reserved trimmings and flesh coarsely. In saucepan of boiling salted water, cook zucchini shells for 2 minutes. Drain and refresh under cold water. Invert shells on paper towels to drain.

■ In skillet, heat oil over medium heat; cook chopped zucchini for 5 minutes or until tender. Stir in parsley, basil and garlic; cook for 1 minute. Transfer to bowl; stir in bread crumbs and egg. Season with salt and pepper to taste.

■ Stuff zucchini shells with bread crumb mixture; place in greased 11- × 7-inch (2 L) baking dish. Pour chicken stock around zucchini; cover and bake in 350°F (180°C) oven for 25 to 30 minutes or until tender and heated through. To serve, spoon some Tomato Salsa on individual plates and top with stuffed zucchini. Garnish with chervil sprigs. Makes 6 servings.

# Sesame Rice

*This dish is also nice with grated orange rind stirred into the rice just before serving. The recipe can be easily doubled.*

| | | |
|---|---|---:|
| 1 tbsp | safflower or vegetable oil | 15 mL |
| 1/4 cup | sesame seeds | 50 mL |
| 1 cup | parboiled rice | 250 mL |
| 1 | onion, chopped | 1 |
| 2 cups | chicken stock | 500 mL |

■ In large saucepan, heat oil over medium-high heat; brown sesame seeds, stirring constantly, for 2 minutes. Add rice and onion; sauté for 3 minutes or until onions are slightly softened.

■ Pour in chicken stock and bring to boil; reduce heat, cover and simmer for about 20 minutes or until rice is tender and liquid is absorbed. Makes 4 servings.

*Sesame Rice; Packets of Fish Fillets with Snow Peas (Easy Main Dishes, p. 49)* ▼

# Leafy Citrus Salad

*When sectioning the fruit, be sure to remove the membranes.*

| | | | | | | |
|---|---|---|---|---|---|---|
| 1 | head romaine lettuce | 1 | | 1/4 tsp | ginger | 1 mL |
| 1 | each orange and grapefruit, peeled and sectioned | 1 | | 1/3 cup | vegetable oil | 75 mL |
| 1 tbsp | sesame seeds | 15 mL | | | Salt and pepper | |

| | DRESSING | |
|---|---|---|
| 2 tbsp | lemon juice | 25 mL |
| 1 tsp | each grated orange and lemon rind | 5 mL |
| 1 tsp | soy sauce | 5 mL |
| 1/2 tsp | Dijon mustard | 2 mL |

■ **Dressing:** In bowl, whisk together lemon juice, orange and lemon rind, soy sauce, mustard and ginger, gradually whisk in oil. Season with salt and pepper to taste.

■ Tear lettuce into bite-size pieces. In bowl, toss lettuce, orange and grapefruit with dressing; sprinkle with sesame seeds. Makes 4 to 6 servings.

# Garlicky Broccoli Pasta

*For a cheesy variation, toss the hot pasta with 1/2 cup (125 mL) freshly grated Parmesan cheese. Recipe can be easily doubled to serve eight.*

| | | |
|---|---|---|
| 1 lb | penne | 500 g |
| 3 cups | broccoli florets | 750 mL |
| 3 tbsp | butter | 50 mL |
| 3 | cloves garlic, minced | 3 |
| | Pepper | |

■ In large pot of boiling salted water, cook pasta for 5 minutes; add broccoli and cook for 3 minutes or until pasta is tender but firm and broccoli tender-crisp.

■ Meanwhile, in small saucepan, heat butter with garlic for 2 to 3 minutes or until garlic is softened. Drain pasta mixture well; turn into warmed bowl. Add garlic butter and toss well; season with pepper to taste. Makes 4 servings.

# Gratin Dauphinoise

*Thin ovals of potatoes, baked in cream with a touch of nutmeg and garlic, are delicious with grilled steaks or chops, or with roast loin of pork or leg of lamb.*

| | | |
|---|---|---|
| 1 | clove garlic, halved | 1 |
| 2 tbsp | butter, softened | 25 mL |
| 5 | large potatoes, peeled (2-1/2 lb/1.25 kg) | 5 |
| 3/4 tsp | salt | 4 mL |
| 1/4 tsp | pepper | 1 mL |
| 1-1/2 cups | shredded Gruyère cheese (6 oz/175 g) | 375 mL |
| 2 | eggs | 2 |
| 1 cup | whipping cream | 250 mL |
| 1 cup | light cream or milk | 250 mL |
| 1/4 tsp | nutmeg | 1 mL |
| 2 tbsp | butter, melted | 25 mL |

■ Rub 6-cup (1.5 L) oval gratin dish with cut sides of garlic; discard garlic. Spread butter over dish.

■ Slice potatoes very thinly lengthwise; let stand in cold water for 5 minutes. Drain and pat dry thoroughly.

■ Arrange one-third of the potatoes in dish, overlapping slices. Sprinkle with one-third of the salt and pepper; top with 1/3 cup (75 mL) of the cheese. Repeat layers; top with remaining potatoes.

■ Beat together eggs, whipping cream and light cream; pour over potatoes. Sprinkle with remaining salt, pepper and remaining cheese; sprinkle with nutmeg, then butter.

■ Bake in 325°F (160°C) oven for 1-1/4 hours or until potatoes are tender and top is crisp and brown. Let stand for 5 minutes. Makes 6 servings.

# Sautéed Zucchini and Cherry Tomatoes

*When zucchini and cherry tomatoes are abundant, this colorful sauté makes an excellent buffet dish.*

| | | |
|---|---|---|
| 12 | small zucchini (2 lb/1 kg) | 12 |
| 1 lb | cherry tomatoes | 500 g |
| 1/4 cup | olive oil | 50 mL |
| 1/2 cup | pine nuts or slivered almonds | 125 mL |
| 2 | cloves garlic, chopped | 2 |
| 1 tsp | salt | 5 mL |
| 1/4 tsp | pepper | 1 mL |
| 1/4 cup | chopped fresh basil | 50 mL |
| 1/2 tsp | granulated sugar | 2 mL |

■ Cut zucchini lengthwise into sticks about 1/4 inch (5 mm) thick. Stem tomatoes.

■ In large skillet, heat half of the oil over medium heat; brown pine nuts lightly. Remove with slotted spoon and set aside.

■ Add half of the garlic and increase heat to high; add zucchini and sauté for about 3 minutes, turning constantly, or just until tender-crisp but not browned. Season with half of the salt and pepper; sprinkle with half of the basil. Transfer to heated oval platter, quickly arranging zucchini in fan shape around edge of platter; cover and keep warm.

■ To skillet, add remaining oil and garlic; sauté tomatoes, shaking pan gently, for about 1-1/2 minutes or until warmed through. Sprinkle with remaining salt, pepper and basil; sprinkle with sugar. Arrange in centre of zucchini; sprinkle circle of pine nuts between zucchini and tomatoes. Serve immediately. Makes 10 servings.

---

*VEGETABLE SAUTÉS*
*A vegetable sauté is an easy and delicious way to serve a side dish. Use any colorful combination you have on hand. Since it should be prepared at the last minute, have all the ingredients ready so the speedy sautéing can be done with a minimum of fuss. You can use a large skillet or wok. Add the longest-cooking vegetables to the pan first, the shortest-cooking ones last and remember not to overcook them.*

---

# Fruit-of-the-Season Salad with Honey Cardamom Sauce

*Combine the unusual flavors of cardamom and rosewater with a variety of winter fruit to liven up a salad course.*

| | | |
|---|---|---|
| 2 | oranges | 2 |
| 2 | bananas | 2 |
| 1 | cantaloupe | 1 |
| 3 | kiwifruit | 3 |
| 1 cup | seedless green grapes | 250 mL |

| | HONEY CARDAMOM SAUCE | |
|---|---|---|
| 1/2 cup | plain yogurt | 125 mL |
| 1 tbsp | honey | 15 mL |
| 1 tbsp | lime juice | 15 mL |
| 1 tsp | rosewater (optional) | 5 mL |
| Pinch | cardamom | Pinch |

■ Peel and section oranges. Peel and thinly slice bananas. Scoop cantaloupe into balls. Peel and thinly slice kiwifruit. In large glass bowl, combine oranges, bananas, cantaloupe, kiwifruit and grapes; set aside.

■ **Honey Cardamom Sauce:** Combine yogurt, honey, lime juice, rosewater (if using) and cardamom; drizzle over salad. Refrigerate for at least 1 hour or up to 8 hours. Makes 6 to 8 servings.

*A FAST AND LIGHT MENU*
*Our crisp Pear, Walnut and Swiss Cheese Salad (opposite page) is perfect alongside savory Beef Creole with Rice (see Easy Main Dishes, p. 32). Warm Plum Compote (see Great Desserts, p. 56) makes a fragrant finale to a healthy dinner fit for family or company.*

# Pear, Walnut and Swiss Cheese Salad

*Also tasty with Cheddar, this salad stars autumn pears such as Bartlett.*

| | | |
|---|---|---|
| 4 | ripe pears | 4 |
| 4 | leaves Boston lettuce | 4 |
| 1/3 cup | chopped walnuts | 75 mL |
| | **DRESSING** | |
| 2/3 cup | plain low-fat yogurt | 150 mL |
| 1/2 cup | shredded Gruyère cheese | 125 mL |
| 1 tbsp | lemon juice | 15 mL |
| 1 tsp | Dijon mustard | 5 mL |

■ **Dressing:** Blend together yogurt, cheese, lemon juice and mustard. Core and thinly slice pears, leaving skin on. Place lettuce leaf on each salad plate; fan pears over lettuce. Spoon dressing over pears; sprinkle with nuts. Serve immediately. Makes 4 servings.

# Couscous Pilaf

*For a large party, this is a terrific make-ahead alternative to rice or pasta and faster to prepare. Even children are crazy about it. Be sure to use the precooked couscous, which is available at Middle Eastern and health food stores and some supermarkets.*

| | | |
|---|---|---|
| 7-1/2 cups | boiling chicken stock | 1.875 L |
| 5 cups | precooked couscous | 1.25 L |
| 1/3 cup | butter | 75 mL |
| 2 | large onions, finely chopped | 2 |
| 2 | cloves garlic, minced | 2 |
| 3 | carrots, finely diced | 3 |
| 1/2 cup | water | 125 mL |
| 2 | cans (each 19 oz/540 mL) chick-peas, drained | 2 |
| 1/2 cup | chopped pistachios or almonds | 125 mL |
| 1/4 cup | chopped fresh parsley | 50 mL |
| | Salt and pepper | |

■ In large saucepan, combine hot chicken stock with couscous; cover and let stand for 15 minutes.

■ Meanwhile, in separate saucepan, melt butter over medium heat; cook onions and garlic for about 8 minutes or until tender. Add carrots and water; cover and cook for 6 minutes.

■ Add chick-peas; reduce heat to medium-low and cook gently for 5 minutes. Add to couscous along with pistachios and parsley. Season with salt and pepper to taste. *(Recipe can be cooled, covered and refrigerated for up to 1 day. Reheat in 350°F/180°C oven for 30 to 40 minutes or until heated through.)* Makes 20 servings.

> *COUSCOUS*
> *Couscous is finely cracked durum wheat or coarse semolina that has been steamed and dried. It is used as a pasta-type food in North African and Moroccan menus.*
>
> • *Plain couscous: In saucepan, bring 1-3/4 cups (425 mL) chicken stock or water to boil. Stir in 1 cup (250 mL) precooked couscous. Cover and let stand for 5 minutes. Fluff with fork. Makes 4 cups (1 L).*
>
> • *You can add chopped toasted nuts, chopped dried fruits, raisins, or sautéed onions or mushrooms to plain couscous for delicious combinations.*

# Fall Greens with Garlic Yogurt Dressing

*In late summer and early fall, light green curly chicory and escarole make a delightful change for salads. A few leaves of radicchio look handsome and add a nice bite.*

| | | |
|---|---|---|
| 1 | heart curly chicory | 1 |
| 1 | heart escarole | 1 |
| 2 | small heads radicchio or Belgian endive | 2 |
| 1 | bunch watercress (or half 10 oz/284 g bag spinach), trimmed | 1 |
| 2/3 cup | shredded Gruyère cheese | 150 mL |

| **DRESSING** | | |
|---|---|---|
| 1 tsp | minced garlic | 5 mL |
| 3/4 tsp | salt | 4 mL |
| 1/2 cup | plain yogurt | 125 mL |
| 1/4 cup | buttermilk | 50 mL |
| 4 tsp | white wine vinegar | 20 mL |
| 1 tbsp | olive oil | 15 mL |
| 1/2 tsp | grainy mustard | 2 mL |
| 1/4 tsp | pepper | 1 mL |

■ Separate leaves of chicory, escarole and radicchio. Break chicory and escarole leaves in two. Wrap each separately in towelling; place in plastic bag and chill.

■ **Dressing:** In small bowl, crush garlic with salt; whisk in yogurt, buttermilk, vinegar, oil, mustard and pepper. Chill at least for 4 hours to allow flavors to blend. Taste and adjust seasoning if necessary.

■ Line large salad bowl with chicory and escarole. Arrange ring of radicchio inside; fill centre with watercress.

■ Sprinkle cheese over chicory and escarole. Drizzle dressing over salad. Makes 10 servings.

# Chunky Braised Squash

*Choose any of the easy-to-peel, fleshy squash — butternut, sweet potato or sweet dumpling — for this harvest supper side dish.*

| | | |
|---|---|---|
| 2 tbsp | butter or olive oil | 25 mL |
| 1 | large onion, chopped | 1 |
| 3 | cloves garlic, minced | 3 |
| 8 cups | cubed peeled squash | 2 L |
| 1/2 tsp | dried thyme or oregano | 2 mL |
| 1/2 cup | chicken stock or dry white wine | 125 mL |
| 1/4 cup | chopped fresh parsley or green onion | 50 mL |
| | Salt and pepper | |

■ In large heavy saucepan, heat butter over medium-low heat; cook onion and garlic until softened, about 4 minutes. Add squash and thyme, mixing well; cook, stirring, for 2 minutes.

■ Pour in stock; cover and cook over very low heat for about 20 minutes or until squash is tender and most of the stock absorbed, stirring gently once or twice. *(Recipe can be prepared to this point, cooled, covered and refrigerated for up to 1 day. Heat through before continuing.)*

■ Gently stir in parsley; season with salt and pepper to taste. Makes about 6 servings.

---

*GRATIN OF BRAISED SQUASH*
*Before adding parsley, salt and pepper, purée squash. Transfer to 13- × 9-inch (3.5 L) baking dish, smoothing top. Cover with mixture of 2 cups (500 mL) fresh whole wheat bread crumbs or cracker crumbs and 1/4 cup (50 mL) melted butter. Bake in 350°F (180°C) oven for about 30 minutes or until heated through and crisp and brown on top.*

# Rhubarb Sour Cream Crunch Pie

*Fresh or frozen rhubarb works equally well in this tangy pie with its crunchy topping. It's at its best when served warm and topped with a scoop of vanilla ice cream.*

| | Pastry for 10-inch (25 cm) single-crust pie | |
|---|---|---|
| 1 | egg | 1 |
| 1 cup | sour cream | 250 mL |
| 1 cup | granulated sugar | 250 mL |
| 3 tbsp | cornstarch | 50 mL |
| 1/2 tsp | cinnamon | 2 mL |
| 1/2 tsp | nutmeg | 2 mL |
| 3 cups | coarsely sliced rhubarb | 750 mL |

| | TOPPING | |
|---|---|---|
| 1/2 cup | rolled oats | 125 mL |
| 1/3 cup | packed brown sugar | 75 mL |
| 1/3 cup | all-purpose flour | 75 mL |
| 1/3 cup | butter, softened | 75 mL |
| 1 tsp | grated orange or lemon rind | 5 mL |

■ On lightly floured surface, roll out pastry and fit into 10-inch (25 cm) pie plate or quiche dish; set aside.

■ In bowl, whisk egg with sour cream. Combine sugar, cornstarch, cinnamon and nutmeg; stir into egg mixture. Stir in rhubarb; spoon into pastry shell.

■ **Topping:** In bowl, combine rolled oats, sugar and flour; cut in butter until crumbly. Stir in orange rind. Sprinkle over rhubarb filling.

■ Bake in 400°F (200°C) oven for 15 minutes. Reduce heat to 375°F (190°C) and bake for 40 to 50 minutes longer or until topping is golden brown and filling is puffed and set. Serve warm. Makes 6 to 8 servings.

# Crumble with Ginger

*...avorite with raisins, chopped walnuts and a generous ...ginger. Serve it hot or cold with a jug of cream, a scoop of ...p of yogurt or sour cream.*

| | | |
|---|---|---|
| 4 cups | ...sliced peeled pears (4 large) | 1 L |
| 4 cups | thinly sliced peeled apples (4 large) | 1 L |
| 1/2 cup | chopped walnuts | 125 mL |
| 1/2 cup | raisins | 125 mL |
| 1/4 cup | packed brown sugar | 50 mL |
| 1/4 cup | chopped preserved ginger | 50 mL |
| 1/2 tsp | ground ginger | 2 mL |
| 1/2 cup | orange juice | 125 mL |
| | **TOPPING** | |
| 3/4 cup | all-purpose flour | 175 mL |
| 1/2 cup | packed brown sugar | 125 mL |
| 1/2 cup | cold butter | 125 mL |

■ In large bowl, stir together pears, apples, walnuts, raisins, sugar, preserved ginger and ground ginger. Spoon into greased 8-cup (2 L) baking dish and smooth top. Drizzle with orange juice.

■ **Topping:** In small bowl, blend flour with sugar; cut in butter until in coarse crumbs. Sprinkle over fruit.

■ Bake in 400°F (200°C) oven for 45 to 55 minutes or until topping is crisp and fruit is tender. Makes 6 to 8 servings.

---

*GREAT GRATINS*

*The French call crusty toppings on dishes "gratins" and they can be used on soups, entrées, side dishes or desserts. For a sweet ending to a meal, make the ever-popular crumble topping with brown sugar, flour and butter. You can spice it up with cinnamon and nutmeg.*

*• The classic gratin dish, made of copper, porcelain or enameled cast iron, is oval and 2 to 3 inches (5 to 7 cm) deep. The shallow pan ensures more crust. But gratin dishes can be round, rectangular or square, and if your cupboards fail to yield an authentic specimen, use a shallow heatproof glass casserole or even a cake pan.*

# Peach Melba Soup

*Serve guests this cool soup for a fabulous finale to an elegant luncheon. If using frozen raspberries, make sure they're unsweetened.*

| | | |
|---|---|---|
| 1/4 cup | water | 50 mL |
| 2 tbsp | granulated sugar | 25 mL |
| 6 cups | sliced peeled peaches | 1.5 L |
| 1-1/2 cups | light cream | 375 mL |
| 1/2 cup | white wine or white grape juice | 125 mL |
| | Vanilla ice cream | |
| | Raspberry Sauce (recipe follows) | |

■ In small saucepan, stir water and sugar over low heat until sugar has dissolved. Let cool.

■ In blender or food processor, combine peaches and 1/2 cup (125 mL) of the cream; purée until smooth. Pour into large bowl; whisk in remaining cream, cooled sugar syrup and wine.

■ Pour into serving bowls. Top with scoop of ice cream; drizzle with Raspberry Sauce. Makes 8 to 10 servings.

### RASPBERRY SAUCE

| | | |
|---|---|---|
| 1 cup | raspberries (fresh or thawed) | 250 mL |
| 1 tbsp | granulated sugar | 15 mL |

■ Pass raspberries through food mill or press through sieve with spoon. Stir in sugar and let stand until sugar has dissolved. Makes about 1 cup (250 mL).

# Lemon Cream Pavé

*Perfect for a crowd, this refreshing dessert can be made up to 2 days ahead. "Pavé" refers to the dessert's flat square shape, imitating tiles or paving stones. If you have time, it's fun to decorate each square differently.*

| | | |
|---|---|---|
| 4 | eggs, separated | 4 |
| 2/3 cup | granulated sugar | 150 mL |
| 1 tbsp | grated lemon rind | 15 mL |
| 1 tbsp | lemon juice | 15 mL |
| 1 tsp | vanilla | 5 mL |
| 2/3 cup | all-purpose flour | 150 mL |

| LEMON RUM SYRUP | | |
|---|---|---|
| 1/3 cup | granulated sugar | 75 mL |
| 1/3 cup | water | 75 mL |
| 2 tbsp | lemon juice | 25 mL |
| 2 tbsp | dark rum | 25 mL |

| LEMON CREAM | | |
|---|---|---|
| 1 | pkg unflavored gelatin | 1 |
| 1/4 cup | cold water | 50 mL |
| 4 | egg yolks | 4 |
| 3/4 cup | granulated sugar | 175 mL |
| 1 tbsp | grated lemon rind | 15 mL |
| 3/4 cup | lemon juice | 175 mL |
| 4 oz | cream cheese, softened | 125 g |
| 1 cup | whipping cream | 250 mL |

| GARNISH | | |
|---|---|---|
| 1-1/2 cups | whipping cream | 375 mL |
| 2 tbsp | sifted icing sugar | 25 mL |
| 2 tbsp | dark rum | 25 mL |
| 10 | strawberries, halved | 10 |
| 2 | kiwifruit, peeled and thinly sliced | 2 |
| 1 | mango, peeled and thinly sliced | 1 |
| 1/2 cup | toasted sliced coconut* | 125 mL |
| 1/4 cup | toasted chopped pistachios* | 50 mL |

■ Grease 15- × 10-inch (40 × 25 cm) jelly roll pan; line with parchment paper. Grease paper and sprinkle lightly with flour. Set aside.

■ In bowl, beat egg yolks with sugar until light and fluffy; beat in lemon rind and juice and vanilla. In separate bowl, beat egg whites until stiff but not dry peaks form; fold into yolk mixture. Gently fold in flour until thoroughly mixed. Spread in prepared pan; bake in 350°F (180°C) oven for 15 to 20 minutes or until golden and cake springs back when lightly touched. Let cool in pan.

■ **Lemon Rum Syrup:** In saucepan, combine sugar, water and lemon juice; bring to boil. Boil for 1 minute; stir in rum. Brush over cake.

■ **Lemon Cream:** In saucepan, sprinkle gelatin over cold water; let stand for 5 minutes to soften. Over low heat, warm gelatin gently just until dissolved.

■ Meanwhile, in bowl, beat egg yolks with sugar until light; beat in lemon rind and juice. Beat in gelatin mixture. Return to saucepan and cook over low heat for 5 to 6 minutes or until barely thickened; let cool slightly.

■ In large bowl, beat cheese until light; beat in lemon mixture. Let cool to room temperature just until starting to thicken. Whip cream; fold into lemon mixture. Spread evenly over cake. Refrigerate for at least 2 hours or up to 2 days. Cut into 20 squares.

■ **Garnish:** Whip cream; beat in sugar and rum. Spoon into pastry bag and pipe decoratively onto each square. Garnish squares attractively with strawberries, kiwifruit, mango, coconut and pistachios. Makes 20 servings. *Toast coconut and pistachios on separate baking sheets in 350°F (180°C) oven for 5 minutes or until golden.

# Walnut Brandy Torte

*This is a light four-layer walnut sponge cake "sandwiched" together with brandy-flavored whipped cream. You can make and chill this for up to 4 hours.*

| 8 | eggs, separated | 8 |
|---|---|---|
| 1/4 tsp | salt | 1 mL |
| 1/4 tsp | cream of tartar | 1 mL |
| 1-1/2 cups | granulated sugar | 375 mL |
| 3 tbsp | brandy | 50 mL |
| 1-1/2 cups | finely ground walnuts | 375 mL |
| | **FILLING** | |
| 2 cups | whipping cream | 500 mL |
| 1 tbsp | icing sugar | 15 mL |
| 1 tbsp | brandy | 15 mL |
| 12 | walnut halves | 12 |

■ Line 15- × 10-inch (40 × 25 cm) jelly roll pan with waxed paper. Grease paper and dust with flour. Set aside.

■ In bowl, beat egg whites until foamy; beat in salt and cream of tartar until soft peaks form. Gradually beat in 1/4 cup (50 mL) of the sugar until stiff peaks form.

■ In large bowl, beat egg yolks with remaining sugar until pale and thickened. Beat in 1 tbsp (15 mL) of the brandy. Stir in one-quarter of the egg white mixture. Fold in remaining egg whites along with nuts.

■ Spread batter in prepared pan. Bake in 350°F (180°C) oven for 35 minutes or until cake springs back when lightly touched. Let cool in pan. Sprinkle with remaining brandy. Cover with waxed paper and damp tea towel; chill for 1 hour.

■ Invert cake onto clean tea towel; remove pan and carefully peel off paper. Trim crusty edges and divide cake evenly into 4 rectangles.

■ **Filling:** Whip cream; stir in icing sugar and brandy. On platter, assemble torte, spreading some of the filling over each layer. Spread remaining filling over top and sides, saving enough to pipe rosettes around bottom. Place walnuts in rosettes. Makes 10 servings.

# Microwave Orange Custard Parfaits

*Easy to prepare, orange-flavored parfaits are a satisfying finale to any special meal.*

| | | |
|---|---|---|
| 1-1/4 cups | milk | 300 mL |
| 1/3 cup | granulated sugar | 75 mL |
| 2 tbsp | cornstarch | 25 mL |
| 2 | egg yolks, beaten | 2 |
| 1/4 cup | orange juice | 50 mL |
| 1 tbsp | grated orange rind | 15 mL |
| 1 tbsp | butter | 15 mL |
| 2 | navel oranges, peeled and sectioned | 2 |
| 1 tbsp | orange liqueur | 15 mL |

■ In 4-cup (1 L) microwaveable measure, combine milk, sugar and cornstarch; microwave at High, uncovered, for 3-1/2 minutes or until slightly thickened, whisking twice.

■ Whisk one-third of the hot milk mixture into egg yolks; return yolk mixture to measure and microwave at High for about 1 minute or until bubbling around edge, whisking once.

■ Stir in orange juice and rind and butter until butter has melted. Place plastic wrap directly on surface of custard; refrigerate for about 2 hours or until chilled.

■ Meanwhile, toss oranges with liqueur; refrigerate until chilled. Divide orange sections among 4 parfait glasses; spoon custard evenly over top. Makes 4 servings.

---

*ORANGE SENSATIONS*

*Nothing could be simpler or more appealing for dessert than an attractive and interesting presentation of this wonderful fruit.*

- *Caramelized Oranges: Sprinkle orange segments or slices with brown sugar and broil.*
- *Cinnamon Orange Compote: Sprinkle orange slices with sugar and cinnamon; drizzle with red wine.*
- *Warm Citrus Sections: Sprinkle orange and grapefruit sections with brown sugar and dot with butter; broil until golden. Sprinkle with toasted coconut and almonds, or granola.*

# Blueberry-Raspberry Gratin

*This is a great dessert for entertaining, needing only a few minutes under the broiler just before serving.*

| | | |
|---------|------------------------|--------|
| 2 tbsp  | butter, softened       | 25 mL  |
| 1/2 cup | granulated sugar       | 125 mL |
| 1 tsp   | cornstarch             | 5 mL   |
| 1       | egg, separated         | 1      |
| 1/2 cup | light cream            | 125 mL |
| 1 tsp   | vanilla                | 5 mL   |
| 2 cups  | blueberries            | 500 mL |
| 2 cups  | raspberries            | 500 mL |
| 1 tbsp  | packed brown sugar     | 15 mL  |

■ In heavy saucepan, blend together butter, all but 1 tbsp (15 mL) of the sugar and cornstarch; whisk in egg yolk and cream. Cook over medium heat, stirring constantly, for 3 minutes or until boiling and thickened. Add vanilla.

■ In bowl, beat egg white until soft peaks form; gradually beat in reserved sugar until stiff glossy peaks form. Fold into cream mixture. *(Custard can be cooled, covered and refrigerated for up to 2 hours.)*

■ Place blueberries and raspberries in 9-inch (23 cm) deep-dish pie plate. Spoon custard over; sprinkle with brown sugar. Broil for 1 to 1-1/2 minutes or until golden. Makes 4 to 6 servings.

---

*BLUEBERRIED TREASURE*
*Blueberries range in size from the small flavorful wild or lowbush variety (found in Quebec, Nova Scotia and New Brunswick) to the larger highbush berries (grown in British Columbia), and in color from soft blue to deep blackish blue. The silvery bloom on the skin of some berries is a natural protective waxy coating. Choose well-colored berries (red or green berries will not ripen) of fairly uniform size. Refrigerate and use within two or three days. Just before serving, wash berries, remove any stems and drain well.*

# Orange Ginger Pudding

*Capture summer with this shimmering cool dessert.*

| | | |
|---|---|---|
| 2 | pkg unflavored gelatin | 2 |
| 1/2 cup | cold water | 125 mL |
| 1 cup | whipping cream | 250 mL |
| 1/2 cup | granulated sugar | 125 mL |
| 3 cups | buttermilk | 750 mL |
| 2 tbsp | chopped candied ginger | 25 mL |
| 1 tsp | grated orange rind | 5 mL |
| 1 tsp | vanilla | 5 mL |
| | **GARNISH** | |
| 1 cup | sliced peeled peaches | 250 mL |
| 1 cup | red raspberries | 250 mL |

■ In top of double boiler, sprinkle gelatin over cold water; let stand for 1 minute to soften. Heat over hot, not boiling, water until dissolved. Add cream and sugar, stirring constantly until sugar dissolves.

■ Remove from heat. Stir in buttermilk, ginger, orange rind and vanilla. Place pan in large bowl of ice water; stir for 5 to 7 minutes or until mixture thickens to consistency of raw egg whites. Pour into 6-cup (1.5 L) mould or 8 individual custard cups. Refrigerate, covered, for several hours or overnight.

■ Unmould pudding onto platter. Garnish with peaches and raspberries. Makes 8 servings.

# Vanilla Pots de Crème with Strawberry Sauce

*Make meringues with the leftover egg whites and freeze them. Serve them with vanilla ice cream and strawberry sauce for another occasion.*

| | | |
|---|---|---|
| 9 | egg yolks | 9 |
| 3/4 cup | granulated sugar | 175 mL |
| 3 cups | whipping cream | 750 mL |
| 1-1/2 tsp | vanilla | 7 mL |
| | Freshly grated nutmeg | |
| 2-1/2 cups | sliced strawberries (or 300 g pkg sliced frozen strawberries) | 625 mL |

■ In large bowl, beat egg yolks until pale and thickened; beat in sugar. Gradually beat in cream; stir in vanilla. Strain through sieve.

■ Pour about 1/3 cup (75 mL) of the mixture into each of 10 small baking dishes or custard cups; sprinkle each with pinch of nutmeg. Place dishes in large baking pan; pour in enough warm water to come halfway up sides. Cover pan with foil; bake in 300°F (150°C) oven for 15 minutes or until knife inserted in centre comes out clean. Let cool to room temperature, then refrigerate.

■ In food processor or blender, purée strawberries; spoon a little over each dessert. Or, run knife around each dessert and unmould onto plates; drizzle with purée. Makes 10 servings.

# Chocolate Ice Cream Pie

*What could be handier or easier than an ice cream pie, waiting in the freezer until guests arrive. Vary ice cream according to your pleasure.*

| | | |
|---|---|---|
| 3 tbsp | butter | 50 mL |
| 1 cup | vanilla wafer crumbs | 250 mL |
| 1/4 cup | finely chopped almonds | 50 mL |
| 2 tbsp | granulated sugar | 25 mL |
| 4 cups | chocolate ice cream | 1 L |
| 1/4 cup | sliced almonds | 50 mL |

■ **Microwave method:** In microwaveable bowl, microwave butter at High for 30 seconds or until melted; mix in wafer crumbs, chopped almonds and sugar. Press onto side and bottom of lightly greased 9-inch (23 cm) pie plate; microwave at High for 1-1/2 minutes or until set. Let cool completely.

■ Microwave ice cream at Medium-Low (30%) for about 1 minute or until softened but not melted. Spoon into crust; cover and freeze until firm, about 1-1/2 hours.

■ Spread sliced almonds evenly over plate; microwave at High for 6 to 8 minutes or until lightly toasted, stirring often. Sprinkle around edge of pie just before serving.

■ **Conventional method:** In saucepan, heat butter until melted; stir in wafer crumbs, chopped almonds and sugar. Press onto bottom and side of lightly greased 9-inch (23 cm) pie plate; bake in 350°F (180°C) oven for about 10 minutes or until golden. Let cool completely.

■ Let ice cream stand at room temperature for about 30 minutes or until softened but not melted. Spoon into crust; cover and freeze until firm, about 1-1/2 hours.

■ Spread almonds on baking sheet; bake in 350°F (180°C) oven for 8 to 10 minutes or until lightly toasted. Sprinkle around edge of pie just before serving.

---

*EASY ICE CREAM DRESS-UPS*
*When you're entertaining on short notice, ice cream makes a fast and easy spur-of-the-moment dessert. Serve it in stemmed glasses or on dessert plates.*
*• Make a quick sauce to pour over the ice cream by puréeing a package of frozen sweetened raspberries or strawberries.*
*• For a simple treat with tropical flavor, purée peeled, fresh peaches and serve over coconut ice cream.*

# Credits

Recipes in THE CANADIAN LIVING COOKING COLLECTION have been created by the *Canadian Living* Test Kitchen and by the following food writers from across Canada: **Elizabeth Baird, Karen Brown, Joanna Burkhard, James Chatto, Diane Clement, David Cohlmeyer, Pam Collacott, Bonnie Baker Cowan, Pierre Dubrulle, Eileen Dwillies, Nancy Enright, Carol Ferguson, Margaret Fraser, Susan Furlan, Anita Goldberg, Barb Holland, Patricia Jamieson, Arlene Lappin, Anne Lindsay, Lispeth Lodge, Mary McGrath, Susan Mendelson, Bernard Meyer, Beth Moffatt, Rose Murray, Iris Raven, Gerry Shikatani, Jill Snider, Kay Spicer, Linda Stephen, Bonnie Stern, Lucy Waverman, Carol White, Ted Whittaker** and **Cynny Willet.**

The full-color photographs throughout are by Canada's leading food photographers, including **Fred Bird, Doug Bradshaw, Christopher Campbell, Nino D'Angelo, Frank Grant, Michael Kohn, Suzanne McCormick, Claude Noel, John Stephens** and **Mike Visser.**

**Editorial and Production Staff**: Hugh Brewster, Susan Barrable, Catherine Fraccaro, Wanda Nowakowska, Sandra L. Hall, Beverley Renahan and Bernice Eisenstein.

# Index

# LOOK FOR THESE BESTSELLING COOKBOOKS FROM *CANADIAN LIVING*

## The most trusted name in Canadian cooking